Thankfulness...

All praise is due to Allaah the Exalted for His Essence and Beautiful Attributes. All thanks are for Allaah for His blessings, bounties, favor, and grants. May Allaah send peace and blessings on His slave and Messenger, the one sent with the sound Religion, our master, chief, and prophet, Muhammad, sallallaahu 'alayhi wa sallam, the trustworthy Messenger, and on his family and Companions, the guided ones who also guide others.

To proceed:

Since faith consists of two halves, the first being thankfulness, and the other being patience, it is important for the person who admonishes their soul, wishes to safeguard it, and prefers its happiness, not to neglect these two great principles, turn away from these two treaded paths, and to make their path and journey to Allaah between these two paths, so that Allaah the Exalted places them, upon their meeting, in the better of the two parties.

Thankfulness is the essential goodness of the lives of those who are happy, who do not ascend to their high ranks through anything besides their thankfulness. They traversed the path between the two wings of patience and thankfulness to the Gardens of Bliss, and that is the bounty of Allaah that He gives whoever He wills, and Allaah possesses great bounties.

Thankfulness is a characteristic of the prophets, may Allaah exalt their mention.

The first Messenger sent to humankind was Nooh (Noah), may Allaah exalt his mention, and Allaah the Exalted described him as being a slave who is oft-thankful. **Allaah the Exalted Says (what means):** {O descendants of those We carried [in the ship] with Noah. Indeed, he was a grateful servant.} [QUR'AAN 17:3] **Specifically mentioning Nooh, may Allaah exalt his mention, shows that we must follow in his footsteps, because he is the second father of humanity, after Adam, may Allaah exalt his mention.**

Abu Hurayrah, may Allaah be pleased with him, reported that Allaah's Messenger, sallallaahu `alayhi wa sallam, said: "I am the chief of people on the Day of Resurrection," **to the end of the Hadeeth, and it also contains:** "They will go to Nooh and say: 'O Nooh, you are the first of the messengers to humankind, and Allaah has called you a slave who is oft-thankful, so, intercede on our behalf.'"[1]

Allaah the Exalted informed about His close friend, Ibraaheem (Abraham), may Allaah exalt his mention, and mentioned that he was thankful for what he was bestowed with (what means): {Indeed, Abraham was a [comprehensive] leader, devoutly obedient to Allaah, inclining toward truth, and he was not of those who associate others with Allaah. [He was] grateful for His favors. Allaah chose him and guided him to a straight path.} [QUR'AAN 16:121]

Also, our Prophet, sallallaahu `alayhi wa sallam, as explained by `Aa'ishah, may Allaah be pleased with her, when she described his thankfulness towards his Lord: "Allaah's

---

[1] Reported by Al-Bukhaari (3340) and Muslim (194)

Messenger, sallallaahu `alayhi wa sallam, used to pray until his feet would crack and split. I said: 'O Allaah's Messenger, are you doing this while Allaah has forgiven your past and future sins?' He said: *'O `Aa'ishah, shall I not be a slave most thankful?'*"[1]

Allaah the Exalted has described that His Pleasure lies in thanking Him, Saying (what means): {And if you are grateful, He approves it for you} [QUR'AAN 39:7]

The Prophet, sallallaahu `alayhi wa sallam, criticized his Companions for not taking the Jinn as examples in their thankfulness. Jaabir, may Allaah be pleased with him, said: "Allaah's Messenger, sallallaahu `alayhi wa sallam, went out to his Companions, and read to them Chapter Ar-Rahmaan from its beginning to its end, and they remained silent. Then, he said: *'I read this to the Jinn during their night, and they had a better reaction than you all had. Everything I came across (what means):* {So which of the favors of your Lord would you deny?} *they would say: 'None of your bounties do we deny, O our Lord, so praise belongs to You.'*"[2]

It is important that we get to know more about the subject of thankfulness. What does it mean? What is its ruling? What are its fruits? What are the means that a person can use to attain it?

---

[1] Reported by Al-Bukhaari (4837) and Muslim (2820)
[2] Reported by At-Tirmithi (3291) and Al-Haakim, may Allaah have mercy on him, ruled it as being authentic, and Ath-Thahabi, may Allaah have mercy on him, agreed with his conclusion, saying: "It is authentic according to the conditions stipulated by Al-Bukhaari and Muslim."

Let us, dear reader, read the following pages. We ask Allaah the Exalted to make us among those who hear sound speech and follow the best of it, and to make us those who thank Him, and do not deny Him. Allaah's Help is sought, and on Him do we rely.

The definition of thankfulness

Linguistically:

Thankfulness is to admit good conduct and promote it. When formed as 'Shakoor,' it means, someone who is very thankful. In Arabic, Shukr (thankfulness) refers to the effect food has on the body of the animal, and when an animal is called Shakoor, it means the animal that fattens with little feed.

When used in certain phrases, it could mean intensity of rain, and when used to describe an udder, it means that it is filled with milk.[1] Therefore, the meanings of thankfulness all revolve around increase and growth.

Terminologically:

Thankfulness is to put effort into doing acts of obedience, abstaining from prohibitions, in public and in private. Some have said that thankfulness is to admit negligence and deficiency in thanking the one who bestows.[2]

---

[1] Lisaan Al-`Arab (4/424)
[2] Tafseer Al-Qurtubi (1/438)

Al-Farraa', may Allaah have mercy on him, said: "Thankfulness is to admit good conduct and speak about it."[1]

Based on that, we say that thankfulness is to show the effects of Divine Bounties on the slave in their heart through faith, on their tongue through praising and thanking Him, and on their limbs by doing acts of worship and obedience.

The difference between praising (Hamd) and thankfulness (Shukr):

Hamd (praise) means to praise someone through statement, due to their inherent and transmittable characteristics. As for thankfulness, it is expressed through the tongue, heart, and limbs, but it only occurs for transmittable characteristics.

Therefore, Hamd is only through speech, and Shukr is through speech, action, and in the heart. Hamd can be used for attributes that are inherent (such as beauty), and transmittable (such as good conduct).

As for Shukr, it only refers to attributes that are transmittable (such as good conduct). At times, both are interchangeable.[2] It is also said that Hamd can be used in place of Shukr, but Shukr cannot be used in place of Hamd.[3]

---

[1] Ibid. (2/166)
[2] Tafseer Ibn Katheer (1/43)
[3] Adab Al-Kitaab (pg. 31)

Factors associated with thankfulness

When we realize that thankfulness is the heart's devotion to loving the one who is bestowing something, the limb's devotion to obeying, and the tongue's consistent mention and praise of them, we realized that thankfulness deals with and is associated with three things: the heart, the tongue, and the limbs.

Thankfulness with the heart:

Thankfulness with the heart is for the person to know that Allaah the Exalted is the One Who bestowed all the bounties that they are basking in. Some people ascribe blessings and bounties to those who gives it to them, such as an individual who is rich or has a high status, but forget Allaah the Exalted who gave the rich person in order for them to give [the poor person]. The rich person, in this instance, is just a means, but Allaah the Exalted is the One that gave. People, unfortunately, thank the means, but not the source!

That is why it is important to teach children where blessings come from, and that Allaah the Exalted is the Source of sustenance, so that the child is brought up thankful to their Lord. Allaah the Exalted Says (what means): {O mankind, remember the favor of Allaah upon you. Is there any creator other than Allaah who provides for you from the heaven and earth? There is no deity except Him, so how are you deluded?} [QUR'AAN 35:3]

After knowing this, the thankful person must love the one giving and bestowing them with apparent and hidden bounties.

Thankfulness with the tongue:

A person's tongue expresses what their heart conceals. If a person's heart is filled with thankfulness to Allaah, the tongue would utter praise and thank to Him. Ponder the supplications of the Prophet, sallallaahu `alayhi wa sallam, and how they consist of praise and thanks to the Lord of all that exists.

> 1. **When the Prophet, sallallaahu `alayhi wa sallam, would wake up, he would say:** "All praise is for Allaah, who has given us life after He has caused us to die, and to Him is the gathering."[1] **He also ordered us to say this supplication:** "All praise is for Allaah, who has made me healthy in my body, given me back my soul, and allowed me to remember Him."[2]
>
> 2. **Anas, may Allaah be pleased with him, reported that Allaah's Messenger, sallallaahu `alayhi wa sallam, when he would go to his bed, would say:** "All praise is for Allaah who has fed us, allowed us to drink, sufficed us, and sheltered us. How many people have no one to suffice or shelter them?"[3]

---

[1] Reported by Al-Bukhaari (6312)
[2] Reported by At-Tirmithi (3401) and Al-Albaani ruled it as being acceptable
[3] Reported by Muslim (2715)

Thankfulness

3. **Abu Umaamah, may Allaah be pleased with him, reported that whenever Allaah's Messenger, sallallaahu `alayhi wa sallam, would finish his meal, he would say:** "All praise is for Allaah who has sufficed us, gave us water, without needing anyone [but everyone is in need of Him], or being shown ungratefulness. All praise is for Allaah, who does not need anyone, is never abandoned [in worship], and can never be dispensed, our Lord."[1]

4. **In the Du`aa' known as the Chief of Repentance, he would say:** "I acknowledge your blessings on me, and I acknowledge my sin."[2]

5. **Among the supplications of night prayer is:** "O Allaah, to You belongs praise. You are the Light of the heavens and earth, and everything in them."[3] Also: "Allaah is truly ever Greatest, all and many praises are for Allaah, and glorified is Allaah by day and by night."[4]

6. **`Aa'ishah, may Allaah be pleased with her, said:** "I was missing Allaah's Messenger, sallallaahu `alayhi wa sallam, one night in bed, and when I felt around for him, my hand touched the bottom of his feet while he was praying, and they were standing up

---

[1] Reported by Al-Bukhaari (5459)
[2] Reported by Al-Bukhaari (6306)
[3] Reported by Al-Bukhaari (1120)
[4] Reported by Abu Dawood (764) and Al-Haakim ruled it as being authentic

straight. He was saying: *"O Allaah, I seek refuge in your Pleasure from your Wrath, in your Forgiveness from your Punishment, and I seek refuge in You from You. I cannot possibly thank you enough, and You are as You praised yourself."*[1]

7. **Also, at the ending of his prayers, he would say, as Mu`aath ibn Jabal, may Allaah be pleased with him, reported, that Allaah's Messenger, sallallaahu `alayhi wa sallam, took his hand and said:** *"O Mu`aath, by Allaah, I love you... do not ever forget or neglect to say at the end of every prayer: 'O Allaah, help me to remember You, thank You, and worship You in a good manner.'"*[2]

Thankfulness with the limbs:

Thankfulness with the limbs occurs by doing good actions. The Qur'aan advises those who have reached the age of forty, saying (what means): *{[He grows] until, when he reaches maturity and reaches [the age of] forty years, he says, 'My Lord, enable me to be grateful for Your favor which You have bestowed upon me and upon my parents and to work righteousness of which You will approve.'}* [QUR'AAN 46:15]
So, he asked Allaah the Exalted for good actions after asking

---

[1] Reported by Muslim (486)
[2] Reported by Abu Dawood (1522) and Al-Haakim ruled it as being authentic, saying that it is authentic according to the conditions stipulated by Muslim.

Him for Divine help in being able to thank Him for His blessings and bounties.

Among the ways of thanking Allaah through the limbs is to give charity on behalf of every joint. Abu Tharr, may Allaah be pleased with him, reported that the Prophet, sallallaahu `alayhi wa sallam, said: "Everyone wakes up with charity due on their joints – however, there are three-hundred and sixty joints, so how can they give their thanks for those joints? – so, every Tasbeeh (saying Subhaan Allaah) is a charity, every Tahmeed [saying Al-Hamdu Lillaah] is a charity, every Tahleel [saying La Ilaaha Illa Allaah] is a charity, every Takbeer [saying Allaahu Akbar] is a charity, every [act of] enjoining good is a charity, and every [act of] forbidding evil is a charity."[1]

Ibn `Abbaas, may Allaah be pleased with him, reported: "Every good word is charity, every time a man helps his brother, it is charity, every time someone gives water to another person to drink, it is charity, and removing harm from the pathway is charity."[2]

There are many types of charity, Ibn Rajab, may Allaah have mercy on him, collected them in his explanation of An-Nawawi's Forty Hadeeth, in a work called Jaami` Al-`Uloom wa Al-Hikam. Among them is gratitude that occurs through

---

[1] Reported by Muslim (720)
[2] Al-Adab Al-Mufrad (422) and Al-Albaani ruled it as being authentic

action, such as what Thu Al-Qarnain did when he built protective walls that would protect those ignorant people.

Also, among ways that one can express gratitude through their limbs is what is known as Sujood Ash-Shukr (prostration of thankfulness). Abu Bakrah, may Allaah be pleased with him, reported that whenever something pleasurable would happen to the Prophet, sallallaahu `alayhi wa sallam, or if he was given glad tidings, he would prostrate in thankfulness to Allaah the Exalted.[1]

When Abu Bakr, may Allaah be pleased with him, was informed about the killing of Muslailimah, the apostate, and one of the most severe people against the Muslims, against whom Abu Bakr, may Allaah be pleased with him, incited the Arabs, he fell in prostration to Allaah the Exalted.[2]

Abu Moosa Al-Hamathaani, may Allaah have mercy on him, said: "I was with `Ali during the Day of Nahrawaan, and he said: 'Search for Thu Ath-Thudyah.' They searched for him, but could not find him. We found him in a small part of a tree trunk or in a creek under some dead people. He was brought to `Ali, and he fell in prostration."[3] The reason he did so was because the Prophet, sallallaahu `alayhi wa sallam, had informed `Ali, may Allaah be pleased with him, that Thu Ath-Thudyah would be with the Khawaarij (rebels).

Also, when Ka`b ibn Maalik, may Allaah be pleased with him, was forgiven by Allaah, he fell in prostration to Allaah the

---

[1] Reported by Abu Dawood (2774) and Al-Albaani ruled it as being authentic
[2] `Awn Al-Ma`bood (7/328)
[3] Musannaf `Abdur-Razzaaq (5962)

Exalted, out of thankfulness.[1] Abu `Abd Rabb, one of the pious predecessors, when his mother became Muslim after the `Asr prayer on Friday, he prostrated until the sun set.[2]

Sujood Ash-Shukr is not legislated for every bounty, but rather, for new bounties. Abu Nasr Al-Arghabaani, may Allaah have mercy on him, said: "Prostration of thankfulness is a voluntary practice when one is surprised with a blessing, or when a calamity or hardship is warded off from them; it is not recommended to do for blessings that are constant."[3]

Zaid ibn Ja`daan, may Allaah have mercy on him, said: "We were with Al-Hasan Al-Basri, and he was concealing himself in the home of Abu Khaleefah Al-`Abadi. A man came and said: 'O Abu Sa`eed, Al-Hajjaaj has died.' At that, he fell in prostration."[4] Also, of the sudden blessings [that a person can and should prostrate for] is when a newborn is born, victory is given in a battle, and so forth.

Prayer combines all three types of thankfulness:

Prayer combines all these three factors associated with thankfulness. It is thankfulness of the heart because of the concentration and sincerity it consists of. It is thankfulness with the tongue because of the recitation of the Qur'aan and remembrance of Allaah the Exalted. It is thankfulness with the

---

[1] Reported by Muslim (2769)
[2] Hilyat Al-Awliyaa' (5/160)
[3] Al-Baa`ith `alaa Inkaar Al-Bida (pg. 61)
[4] Fadheelat Ash-Shukr by Al-Kharaati'i (pg. 66)

limbs because of the prostration, bowing, bending, etc. therefore, holding fast to prayer is a way to give thanks to Allaah the Exalted.

The three meanings of thankfulness

The meaning of thankfulness includes knowing three things, and they are the three meanings of thankfulness.

First: To know the blessing: Meaning, to acknowledge and distinguish it in one's mind. A Muslim, through knowing the blessing, gets to know the One giving the blessing. When the person knows the One giving, they love Him. When they love Him, they show seriousness in seeking and thanking Him. This is how worship is achieved, because it is a way to thank the One who bestows, that is, Allaah the Exalted.

Second: Accepting and taking the gift: The slave should be content with what Allaah the Exalted has specifically set for them as blessing and bounty. They should not think that the bounty given to them is low in stature or position.

Third: Praising the One who gave: It is of two types:

1. **General:** Meaning, to describe Him as being generous, benevolent, having good conduct, showing care, and so forth.
2. **Specific:** Meaning, to tell about what He has bestowed on you, and how it reached you. Allaah the Exalted Says (what means): {But as for the favor of your Lord, report [it].} [QUR'AAN 93:11]

There are two opinions as to what speaking about the blessings means in this verse.

1. It means to use those things in obedience of Allaah the Exalted.
2. It means to mention and enumerate the blessings that Allaah the Exalted has bestowed on you, by saying: 'Allaah has blessed me with this, that, and so forth.' That is why some exegetes said in explaining the verse, that it means mention the things that He has bestowed on you in this Chapter, such as helping you when you were an orphan, guiding you after you were misguided, and making you rich after you were poor.

Abu Rajaa' Al-`Ataaridi, may Allaah have mercy on him, said: "`Imraan ibn Husain came out to us wearing a silk shawl that we had not seen before – meaning, it was very expensive clothing – and he said: 'Allaah's Messenger, sallallaahu `alayhi wa sallam, said: *Whoever Allaah the Exalted bestows a blessing on, Allaah loves to see the effect of His blessing on His slave.*"[1]

An-Nu`maan ibn Basheer, may Allaah be pleased with him, said: "Allaah's Messenger, sallallaahu `alayhi wa sallam, said while on the pulpit: *Whoever does not thank for the little does not thank for the much, and whoever does not thank*

---

[1] Reported by Ahmad (19948) and Al-Albaani ruled it as being authentic

Thankfulness

the people has not thanked Allaah. Speaking about Allaah's blessings is a way of showing thankfulness, and abandoning [speaking about it] is ingratitude. The congregation is mercy, and disunity is punishment."[1]

The Prophet, sallallaahu `alayhi wa sallam, said: "Eat, drink, give charity, and wear [good clothing] as long as it is not out of arrogance or extravagance. Allaah the Exalted loves that His favor on His slave is seen."[2] **Al-Hasan, may Allaah have mercy on him, said: "Always mention these blessings, because mentioning them is a way of showing thankfulness."**[3]

The rule of speaking about what Allaah the Exalted has bestowed:

Creation, in speaking about blessing, is of three types:

1. **Someone who thanks for the blessing and praises the One who gave it to them.**
2. **Someone who denies and hides it.**
3. **Someone who makes it seem that they are of those with many blessings, when in fact they are not.**

Some ignorant people think that speaking about the blessings of Allaah is to buy the most expensive clothes, drive the most luxurious cars, and eat the best and most expensive foods. That is a grave mistake, because speaking about Allaah's

---

[1] Reported by Ahmad (18472) and Al-Albaani ruled it as being acceptable
[2] Reported by Ahmad (6708) and Shu`aib Al-Arnaa'oot ruled it as being acceptable
[3] Shu`ab Al-Imaan (4421)

blessings is something through which Allaah the Exalted grants you sustenance. If Allaah the Exalted gives you abundant goodness, then you should dress and buy in a manner that shows Allaah's favors on you. If Allaah the Exalted gives you just enough to satisfy your provisions and family and did not give you much else, then you buy what is in accordance with what Allaah the Exalted has given you, and do not go beyond what you can bear.

Allaah's Messenger, sallallaahu `alayhi wa sallam, said: *"The one who dresses in a manner that they cannot afford is like someone who wears two deceptive garments."*[1] **Abu Al-Ahwas reported that his father said: "I went to Allaah's Messenger, sallallaahu `alayhi wa sallam, in a ragged looking state. He said to me:** *'Do you have wealth?'* **I said: 'Yes.' He said:** *'What kind of wealth?'* **I said: 'Everything; camels, slaves, horses, and goats. 'He said:** *'If Allaah has given you wealth, then let it be shown on you.'"*[2]

Therefore, it is clear that speaking about the blessing is if Allaah the Exalted gave you wealth.

When do you speak about the bounty?

The injunction of speaking about the bounty is to be done in the presence of righteous people. However, if the person is

---

[1] Reported by Al-Bukhaari (4921) and Muslim (2129)
[2] Reported by Ahmad (15929) and Al-Haakim ruled it as authentic by Al-Haakim and Ath-Thahabi agreed with his conclusion

with envious people, then hiding those bounties is not a form of ingratitude, because they did not avoid mentioning it out of stinginess and negligence with regards to Allaah's Right, but rather, to close the door to an evil, as in envy, such as the person who casts the evil eye. It is a form of protection from such a person, their plot, and harms. Also, doing away with harms is from the intents of the Sharee`ah (legislation).

The way to show thankfulness

Thankfulness on part of the slave for the blessings of Allaah is only completed through five things:

1. Submission to Him, and submission of the thankful to the one being thanked. Al-Baidhaawi, may Allaah have mercy on him, said: "The pillar of thanking for blessings is to use it in whatever it was created for, and showing submission to the One who gave it."[1]
2. Loving Him, the Exalted; meaning the thankful should love the One they are thanking.
3. Acknowledging and affirming His bounty.
4. Praising Him because of it.
5. To not use the bounty in what He dislikes, rather, using it in what He likes. Muhammad ibn Ka`b, may Allaah have mercy upon him, said:

---

[1] Tafseer Al-Baidhaawi (pg. 164)

"Thankfulness is to have fear of Allaah and act in obedience of Him."[1]

Ibn Al-Qayyim, may Allaah have mercy on him, said:

"The root of thankfulness is to acknowledge the blessing of the One who bestowed in a way that shows submission, humility, and love. Whoever does not know the blessing, rather, is ignorant of it, cannot be thankful for it. Whoever knows it but does not inform of it, is also not thankful. Whoever knows of the blessing and the one giving the blessing, but denies it by denying that the Bestower even bestowed anything, then they, too have not been thankful.

Further, whoever acknowledges what is being bestowed, as well as the One bestowing it, and does not deny it, but does not submit to, love, be pleased with and through, then they, too, have not been thankful. Also, whoever acknowledges it and the One giving it, admits it, and submits to the One giving through it, as well as loves the One giving and is happy with and through them, and uses it in what [the One giving] loves and in obedience to them, then that person is the true thankful person."[2]

The levels of thanking Allaah:

---

[1] Tafseer At-Tabari (10/354)
[2] Fat-h Al-Majeed (pg. 427)

A very important issue in this regard is that if blessings vary in their extent, then does thankfulness also vary? Yes, thankfulness also varies on part of the slave. As long as the blessing is more abundant, then thankfulness to Allaah the Exalted must also increase.

Reciprocity of bounties:

Thanking Allaah the Exalted is not out of reciprocity, because reciprocating a blessing is impossible. Allaah the Exalted cannot be reached by His slaves, as He the Exalted Says (what means): {Their meat will not reach Allaah, nor will their blood.} [QUR'AAN 22:37]

It is narrated that Dawood (David), may Allaah exalt his mention, said: "O Lord, how can I thank you, when my thanking you is a blessing that You have given me?" Allaah the Exalted Said (what means): "You have now thanked me, O Dawood." Meaning, you have thanked Me once you have acknowledged that you are deficient in being thankful towards the Bestower.[1]

Ash-Shaafi`i, may Allaah have mercy on him, said: "All praise is for Allaah who cannot be thanked for one of His blessings except through a new blessing that necessitates that the slave thank Him through."[2]

---

[1] Tafseer Ibn Katheer (2/711)
[2] Ibid.

Thankfulness

All praise is for Allaah the Exalted who did not hold us accountable for reciprocating bounties. Rather, He forgave us and had mercy on our weakness. He, the Exalted, gave us abundant bounties, and has accepted meager thanks on our behalf. Sulaimaan At-Taimi, may Allaah have mercy on him, said: "Allaah bestowed on His slaves in accordance with His Ability, and held them accountable for thanking Him in accordance with theirs."[1]

The ruling of thankfulness

Thankfulness is one of the most emphasized obligations that are enjoined on the Muslim. The Muslim must know it, reflect on it, and realize its meanings within themselves. There are many evidences that show that thankfulness is obligatory. Among those evidences are:

Direct orders that one be thankful:

Allaah the Exalted Says (what means): {So remember Me; I will remember you. And be grateful to Me and do not deny Me.} [QUR'AAN 2:152] **This verse contains an explicit and direct order that one should be thankful, and an order necessitates that it is obligatory.**
Allaah the Exalted also Says (what means): {And We have enjoined upon man [care] for his parents. His mother carried

---

[1] Ash-Shukr by Ibn Abu Ad-Dunyaa (8)

him, [increasing her] in weakness upon weakness, and his weaning is in two years. Be grateful to Me and to your parents; to Me is the [final] destination.} [QUR'AAN 31:14]

The Prophet, sallallaahu `alayhi wa sallam, was asked: "What type of wealth should we acquire?" He said:
"One of you should have a thankful heart, a tongue that often remembers Allaah, and a wife that helps him in terms of his Hereafter."[1]

Dispraise of those who are not thankful:

Allaah the Exalted Says (what means): {That they may eat of His fruit. And their hands have not produced it, so will they not be grateful?} [QUR'AAN 36:35] **Al-Baidhaawi, may Allaah have mercy on him, said in explaining this verse: "It contains an order that one be thankful, since it contains a censure of those who are not thankful."**[2]

The prophets were ordered to be thankful:

Thankfulness is an act of worship that was not only obliged on this nation, rather, nations that have come before us have been ordered to be thankful. Allaah the Exalted mentioned that He ordered the prophets to be thankful, Saying (what means):

---

[1] Reported by Ibn Maajah (1856) and Al-Albaani ruled it as being authentic
[2] Tafseer Al-Baidhaawi (pg. 433)

{[Allaah] said: 'O Moses, I have chosen you over the people with My messages and My words [to you]. So take what I have given you and be among the grateful.'} [QUR'AAN 7:144]

Worship has been linked to thankfulness:

Allaah the Exalted clarified that worship is linked to thankfulness; whoever is thankful is a worshipper of Allaah, and whoever is not as such is not a worshipper. Allaah the Exalted Says (what means): {Be grateful to Allaah if it is [indeed] Him that you worship.} [QUR'AAN 2:172]

Clarification that the purpose behind creation and being granted command is thankfulness:

Allaah the Exalted informed that Shukr is the purpose of creation and being granted command. As for it being the purpose of creation, it is when Allaah the Exalted Says (what means): {And Allaah has extracted you from the wombs of your mothers not knowing a thing, and He made for you hearing and vision and intellect that perhaps you would be grateful.} [QUR'AAN 16:78] **Allaah the Exalted clarified that He removed them from the wombs of their mothers, gave them hearing, vision and hearts in order that they be thankful.**
As for it being the purpose behind being granted command, Allaah the Exalted Says (what means): {And already had Allaah given you victory at [the battle of] Badr while you were few in number. Then fear Allaah ; perhaps you will be

grateful.} [QUR'AAN 3:123] **He the Exalted clarified that He ordered them to be pious in order that they be thankful. Therefore, thankfulness is the purpose of creation, and the purpose of commandments; humankind was created to thank, and was ordered so that they could thank.**

Ingratitude is mentioned in a dispraised way:

Allaah the Exalted censured ingratitude in many instances in the Qur'aan; Allaah the Exalted Says (what means): *{Then in falsehood do they believe, and in the favor of Allaah they disbelieve?}* [QUR'AAN 29:67] **What can be understood from this dispraise is that one must do the opposite [of what was censured], meaning, be thankful. Through this, the obligated nature of thankfulness is apparent and manifest.**

People are divided into thankful and unthankful people:

Allaah the Exalted divided people into two categories. The first category is one that is thankful, and another that is unthankful; there is no third category. Allaah the Exalted Says (what means): *{Indeed, We guided him to the way, be he grateful or be he ungrateful.}* [QUR'AAN 76:3]

At the death of the Prophet of Islaam, sallallaahu `alayhi wa sallam, Allaah the Exalted informed that people are of two categories: ungrateful people who turned back on their heels, and a believer who is thankful and content with what Allaah the Exalted has decreed. In the same instance, He the Exalted censured the unthankful and praised the thankful. Allaah the

Exalted Says (what means): {Muhammad is not but a messenger. [Other] messengers have passed on before him. So if he was to die or be killed, would you turn back on your heels [to unbelief]? And he who turns back on his heels will never harm Allaah at all; but Allaah will reward the grateful.} [QUR'AAN 3:144]

Through such categorization, the obligation of thankfulness is evident, because ingratitude is forbidden and unlawful, and is one of the most hated things to Allaah, and He is not pleased with it for people. Allaah the Exalted Says (what means): {And if you are grateful, He approves it for you.} [QUR'AAN 39:7]

Factors that lead to thankfulness

The Noble Qur'aan and Prophetic Sunnah lead us to ways by treading upon which we can reach thankfulness to Allaah the Exalted for His Blessings and Favors. Some of those matters are:

Looking at those who are below you:

Abu Hurayrah, may Allaah be pleased with him, reported that Allaah's Messenger, sallallaahu `alayhi wa sallam, said: "Look to those who are below you, not to those who are above you, *because it is more likely that you do not belittle Allaah's blessings on you.*"[1]

Al-Hasan, may Allaah have mercy on him, said: "When Adam was shown his children, he saw that some of them were more favored than others, and he said: 'O Lord, if only you were to make them equal.' He the Exalted replied: 'O Adam, I love to be thanked; the one with more blessings would see their blessings and would praise and thank Me.'"[2]

Ibn Al-Qayyim, may Allaah have mercy on him, said:
"Allaah the Exalted loves to be thanked, and must be thanked, as necessitated by intellect, legislation, and one's innate sound disposition. The obligation of thanking Him is more apparent and inherent than any other obligation. How can it not be obligatory on the slave to praise Him, unify Him, mention His favors and good care, glorify Him, exalt Him, submit to Him, speak of His blessings, and acknowledge His blessings, by all the means that make something obligatory?
Thankfulness is the most beloved thing to Him, and it has a great reward. Because of it, He created creation, revealed books, and legislated religions which necessitates that He creates means through which thankfulness is more complete. An example is that He created differences between His slaves in their manifest and hidden characteristics: He caused them to vary in

---

[1] Reported by At-Tirmithi (2513) and he ruled it as being authentic
[2] Musannaf Ibn Abu Shaibah (35227)

their creation, manners, religions, sustenance, lives, and lifespans. That way, if someone healthy saw someone sick, someone rich saw a poor person, or a believer saw a disbeliever, they would have greater thanks of Allaah, would know the status of His Blessings on them and how He the Exalted specified and assigned virtue to them apart from others. Through this, they increase in thankfulness, submission, and acknowledgement of the blessing."[1]

One of the things that prevents a slave from abandoning thankfulness is when they see someone above them, they should know and believe that it is destiny set by Allaah, and that Allaah the Exalted is the One Who divided people in such a manner, because some people, if they see those who are better off than them, do not thank Allaah. They should know that **Allaah the Exalted Says (what means):** {And it is He who has made you successors upon the earth and has raised some of you above others in degrees [of rank] that He may try you through what He has given you.} [QUR'AAN 6:165]

Remember the blessings of Allaah the Exalted:

Allaah's blessings that He has given to the slave are innumerable; Allaah the Exalted Says (what means): {And if you should count the favors of Allaah, you could not enumerate them.} [QUR'AAN 16:18]

---

[1] Shifaa' Al-'Aleel (pg. 221)

Thankfulness

If the slave remembers those blessings, it would drive and urge them to thank Allaah the Exalted; Ash-Shawkaani, may Allaah have mercy on him, said: "Remembering blessings is a means that causes a person to be thankful for it."[1]

Likewise, ignorance is a cause for lack of thankfulness; Al-Ghazaali, may Allaah have mercy on him, said: "The path of thankfulness was closed to creation due to their ignorance of the kinds of blessings [they bask in], both apparent and hidden, and both in specific and in general."[2]

The first blessing that Allaah the Exalted has bestowed on His creation is that He created us and made us alive; He did not leave us dead. Then, He bestowed His favor on them by making them humans; He did not make us inanimate or animals. Then, He favored us by giving us Islaam and faith; He did not make us Jews, Christians, or Buddhists.

Then, He bestowed His favor on us by granting us guidance; He did not make us sinful or misguided Muslims. Then, He the Exalted bestowed His favor on us by making us people of Sunnah (tradition) and Jamaa`ah (congregation); He did not make us from the deviant sects.

If you know, dear Muslim, that all of these are blessings from Allaah the Exalted for you, it would be appropriate if you thanked Him, remembered Him, turned to Him, repented to Him, and obeyed Him with all types of obedience.

Reminding general folk about the blessings of Allaah the Exalted on them is important in calling to Allaah. Look at the

---

[1] Fat-h Al-Qadeer (2/317)
[2] Ihyaa' `Uloom Ad-Deen (4/126)

sun, and how Allaah the Exalted has created it in this place, and how it rises at certain times. Also, if it were to be further from earth, it would become frozen, and if it were to be closer, it would burn creation.

Look at the moon and how if it was closer, the tide would increase, causing the whole world to drown, but if it went away, the whole earth would be barren.

Reflect on how if there was no atmosphere, how would we be able to protect ourselves from harmful rays?

Among the blessings of Allaah the Exalted on you, O son of Adam, is that He distinguished humankind by creating them with His Hand, apart from all other creation. Allaah the Exalted Says (what means): {[Allaah] said: 'O Iblees [the devil], what prevented you from prostrating to that which I created with My hands? Were you arrogant [then], or were you [already] among the haughty?'} [QUR'AAN 38:75]

Reflect on the cosmic signs that Allaah the Exalted has bestowed on you.

Allaah the Exalted Says (what means):

- {Do you not see that Allaah has made subject to you whatever is in the heavens and whatever is in the earth and amply bestowed upon you His favors, [both] apparent and unapparent?} [QUR'AAN 31:20]

- {It is Allaah who created the heavens and the earth and sent down rain from the sky and produced thereby some fruits as provision for you and subjected for you the ships to sail through the sea by His command and subjected for you the rivers. And He subjected for you the sun and the moon, continuous [in orbit], and subjected for you the night and the day. And He gave you from all you asked of Him. And if you should count the favor of Allaah, you could not enumerate them. Indeed, mankind is [generally] most unjust and ungrateful.} **[QUR'AAN 14:32-34]**

Allaah the Exalted Says in Chapter An-Nahl, which is also called the Chapter of Blessings, because of how many blessings are mentioned in it (what means): {And it is He who subjected the sea for you to eat from it tender meat and to extract from it ornaments which you wear. And you see the ships plowing through it, and [He subjected it] that you may seek of His bounty; and perhaps you will be grateful. And He has cast into the earth firmly set mountains, lest it shift with you, and [made] rivers and roads, that you may be guided. And landmarks. And by the stars they are [also] guided. Then is He who creates like one who does not create? So will you not be reminded? And if you should count the favors of Allaah , you could not enumerate them. Indeed, Allaah is Forgiving and Merciful.} **[QUR'AAN 16:14-18]**

Allaah the Exalted Says (what means): {And Allaah has made for you, from that which He has created, shadows and has made for you from the mountains, shelters and has made for you garments which protect you from the heat and garments which protect you from your [enemy in] battle. Thus does He complete His favor upon you that you might submit [to Him].} [QUR'AAN 16:81]

Also, from Allaah's Blessings on us is that He completed the religion. Allaah the Exalted Says (what means): {This day I have perfected for you your religion and completed My favor upon you and have approved for you Islam as religion.} [QUR'AAN 5:3]

Misguidance of some people has led them to ascribe the blessings of Allaah the Exalted to themselves, their intelligence, and their ability, as Qaaroon did, saying (what means): {I was only given it because of knowledge I have.} [QUR'AAN 28:78]

Either that, or they ascribe them to some devices, as some ignoramuses do today. Allaah the Exalted Says (what means):

- {And whatever you have of favor - it is from Allaah.} [QUR'AAN 16:53]

- {And have you seen the water that you drink? Is it you who brought it down from the clouds, or is it We who bring it down? If We willed, We could make it bitter, so why are you not grateful?} [QUR'AAN 56:68-70]

Some people find a certain dilemma to be problematic, which is that some of the pious predecessors are narrated to have said that they wished they were dead and that Allaah never created

them. Or, that they were trees, and so forth, and they think that this is a form of not acknowledging Allaah's blessing of being created and given life.

The truth is that those Salaf were the peak of thankfulness, but were overtaken by fear, at times, and wished that they had never have been born into this life, so that they are not held accountable. It was not from their custom to wish that they were not alive, at all.

The slave should know that they will be questioned about their blessings:

The slave should know that they will be asked about their blessings. Allaah the Exalted Says (what means): {Then you will surely be asked that Day about pleasure.} [QUR'AAN 102:8] If the person knows that they will be questioned about their blessings on the Day of Resurrection, and that they are accountable for it, including cold water, they would rush to thank Allaah the Exalted out of fear that they are held accountable!

People deviate in understanding this issue, and in turn, they prevent themselves from enjoying blessings so that they are not asked about them on the Day of Resurrection. Allaah the Exalted is pleased that we enjoy them, and ordered us to be thankful for them. Allaah the Exalted Said (what means): {Eat and drink from the provision of Allaah, and do not commit abuse on the earth, spreading corruption.} [QUR'AAN 2:60] **Allaah the Exalted Says (what means):** {O you who have *believed, eat from the good things which We have provided for you and be grateful to Allaah if it is [indeed] Him that you worship.}* [QUR'AAN 2:172]

Actually, gratitude for these blessings only occurs after enjoying them. Some people forbid themselves from enjoying some blessings, but enjoy bigger blessings in spite of that. A man came to Al-Hasan Al-Basri, may Allaah have mercy on him, and said: "I have a neighbor who does not eat Faaloothaj (a type of sweet made from wheat and sugar)." He said: "Why not?"He said: "He said it is because he is not thankful enough for it." Al-Hasan, may Allaah have mercy upon him, said: "Does he drink cold water?" He said: "Yes." Al-Hasan, may Allaah have mercy upon him, said: "Your neighbor is an ignoramus, because Allaah's favor on him in his cold water is greater [than what he is abandoning]."[1]

Further, we say to such people that there are some blessings that you cannot possibly be deprived of, such as breathing, heartbeats, and blood flow, so are you able to be thankful for them? If they say that they are unable to be thankful for them, we say to them that a person cannot possibly fully thank Allaah for His favors on them. Instead, they should enjoy the favor, acknowledge it, then acknowledge that they are deficient, as the Prophet, sallallaahu `alayhi wa sallam, used to say: *"I acknowledge your blessings on me, and I acknowledge my sin."*[2]

---

[1] Tafseer Al-Qurtubi (6/243)
[2] Reported by Al-Bukhaari (5947)

In summary, whoever deprives themselves of delights, and does not eat them without a legislated reason is censured and is innovating. Also, whoever eats delicacies without performing obligatory thanks is censured. As for the people who follow the truth, they enjoy delights without extravagance, and try to be thankful for them.[1]

Asking Allaah the Exalted to help us be thankful:

Among the means is to call on Allaah the Exalted to help us be thankful, by saying: "O Allaah, help me to remember You, thank You, and worship You in a good manner."[2]

Knowing that Allaah the Exalted loves to be thanked:

> Qataadah, may Allaah have mercy on him, said: "Your Lord grants favors, and loves to be thanked."[3]

---

[1] Majmoo' Al-Fataawaa (32/212)
[2] Reported by Abu Dawood (1522) and Al-Haakim ruled it as being authentic, saying that it is authentic according to the conditions stipulated by Muslim.
[3] Tafseer At-Tabari (6/218)

The fruits of thankfulness

Thankfulness has fruits and many benefits. None of these fruits benefit Allaah, rather, all of them go back to the slave in question.

If the slave is grateful, they are doing so for the good of their own selves, and if they are ungrateful, then they do so to their own selves.

Sulaimaan (Solomon), may Allaah exalt his mention, said: as Allaah the Exalted informed of him (what means):

{This is from the favor of my Lord to test me whether I will be grateful or ungrateful. And whoever is grateful, his gratitude is only for [the benefit of] himself. And whoever is ungrateful, then indeed, my Lord is Free of need and Generous.} [QUR'AAN 27:40]

Among the benefits and fruits of thankfulness are:

Being saved from Allaah's punishment:

Allaah the Exalted has clarified in His Book that He does not benefit from punishing creation if they are thankful and believe in Him. Allaah the Exalted Says (what means): {What would Allaah do with your punishment if you are grateful and believe? And ever is Allaah Appreciative and Knowing.} [QUR'AAN 4:147]

Ibn Jareer, may Allaah have mercy on him, said: "Allaah the Exalted does not punish a thankful or a believing person."[1] **Al-Hasan Al-Basri, may Allaah have mercy on him, said: "Allaah allows people to bask in favors for as long as He wills, and if they do not thank Him, He turns it into punishment."**[2]

It is a means to attain Allaah's pleasure:

Anas ibn Maalik, may Allaah be pleased with him, said that Allaah's Messenger, sallallaahu `alayhi wa sallam, said: "Allaah is pleased by a slave that eats some food and thanks Him for it, and drinks some drink and thanks Him for it."[3]

Being distinguished with the blessing of guidance:

Allaah the Exalted mentioned that those who thank Him are singled out with His blessing of guidance, apart from other slaves.
Allaah the Exalted Says (what means): {And thus We have tried some of them through others that the disbelievers might say, 'Is it these whom Allaah has favored among us?' Is not Allaah most knowing of those who are grateful?} [QUR'AAN 6:53]

---

[1] Tafseer At-Tabari (4/338)
[2] Ash-Shukr by Ibn Abu Ad-Dunya (17)
[3] Reported by Muslim (2734)

Ibn Jareer, may Allaah have mercy on him, said: "Allaah the Exalted is Saying: 'I know who from My slaves are thankful for My favors, and those who are unthankful. So, My favor on those whom I have favored with guidance is the recompense of their thankfulness to me for my favors. My humiliation of those who I have led astray from the guided path is a punishment for their ingratitude towards Me."[1]

Preserving the blessing:

Thankfulness is what safeguards blessings from everything that is a means to its destruction and loss. That is why some scholars called thankfulness 'the chain of blessings,' because it chains the blessing, causing it to neither break loose nor flee. `Umar ibn `Abdul-`Azeez, may Allaah have mercy upon him, said: "Restrict and tie the blessings of Allaah the Exalted through thanking Allaah."[2]

Increase:

Allaah the Exalted, in His Noble Book, promised those who are thankful that He will increase them. He the Exalted Says (what means): {And [remember] when your Lord proclaimed, 'If you are grateful, I will surely increase you [in favor]; but if you deny, indeed, My punishment is severe.'} [QUR'AAN 14:7]

---

[1] Tafseer At-Tabari (5/204)
[2] Shu`ab Al-Imaan (4546)

Thankfulness

Therefore, blessings are increased through thankfulness, and are safeguarded from being lost through thankfulness.

Al-Hasan, may Allaah have mercy on him, said: "It has reached me that Allaah, when He blesses and bestows on a people, asks them to thank Him. If they do, He is Able to increase them, but if they are ungrateful, He is Able to turn their blessing into a punishment."[1]

Ar-Rabi` ibn Anas, may Allaah have mercy on him, said: "Allaah remembers those who remember Him, increases those who thank Him, and punishes those who disbelieve and are ungrateful to Him."[2] **That is why they used to call thankfulness two names, 'the preserver,' because it preserves the blessings that are available, and, 'the attracter,' because it attracts blessings that are not available.**[3]

Its reward is not connected to Allaah's Will:

Allaah the Exalted has connected many rewards to His Will. For example, He the Exalted Says about answering supplications (what means): {No, it is Him [alone] you would invoke, and He would remove that for which you invoked Him if He willed.} [QUR'AAN 6:41] **Also, He the Exalted Says about forgiveness (what means):** {He forgives whom He wills and punishes whom He wills.} [QUR'AAN 3:129] **He the Exalted also**

---

[1] Shu`ab Al-Imaan (4536)
[2] Tafseer At-Tabari (2/39)
[3] `Uddat As-Saabireen (pg. 98)

Says about sustenance (what means): {And Allaah gives provision to whom He wills.} [QUR'AAN 2:212] **He the Exalted also Says about repentance (what means):** {And Allaah turns in forgiveness to whom He wills.} [QUR'AAN 9:15] **However, when it came to thankfulness, He left it wide open, saying (what means):** {And we will reward the grateful.} [QUR'AAN 3:145] **He also Says in another verse (what means):** {Allaah will reward the grateful.} [QUR'AAN 3:144] **He the Exalted did not say that He will give them recompense if He wills or that if He wills, He will give them recompense.**

Those who are thankful adorn themselves with Allaah's Descriptions:

Allaah the Exalted named Himself as the Thankful and as being very Thankful. He the Exalted also described those who thank Him with the same description, therefore, He gave them from His description and called them by His Own Name. This is enough to prove how loved and virtuous those who are thankful are.[1]

Supplication is answered:

It was said to Ibraaheem ibn Ad-ham, may Allaah have mercy on him:"Why do we supplicate, but are not answered?" He said: "Because you knew Allaah, but did not obey Him. You knew the Messenger, but did not follow his Sunnah. You knew

---

[1] Madaarij As-Saalikeen (2/242-244)

the Qur'aan but did not act on it. You consumed the blessings of Allaah but did not adequately thank Him for them. You knew Paradise but did not seek it. You knew the Hellfire but did not run from it. You knew Satan but did not fight him, rather, you agreed and followed him. You knew of death but did not prepare for it. You buried the dead but did not take heed. Lastly, you forgot about your own faults, but instead, engaged in the faults of others."[1]

Thanking people

Our Islaamic legislation has ordered us to thank people for their good conduct and favors over us, and the most specific of such orders is that we were ordered to thank our parents. Allaah the Exalted Says (what means): {Be grateful to Me and to your parents.} [QUR'AAN 31:14]

The scholars said: "Those who are most deservingof thanks, good conduct, devotion, obedience, and submission, after the Creator, the Bestowing One, are those whom Allaah has coupled good conduct to along with worshipping and obeying Him, and coupled thanking them with thanking Him, and they are the parents."[2]

Likewise, the Prophet, sallallaahu `alayhi wa sallam, ordered that you thank everyone who did something good for you. In the Hadeeth of Jaabir, may Allaah be pleased with him, he

---

[1] Tafseer Al-Qurtubi (2/303)
[2] Tafseer Al-Qurtubi (5/171)

reported that the Prophet, sallallaahu `alayhi wa sallam, said: "Whoever was given something, and they had the ability to recompense, should recompense what they were given. If they do not have anything to recompense with, they should praise them for what they did. Whoever praises for what they did has thanked them, and whoever hides what they did has been ungrateful."[1]

If you cannot find anything to give in recompense, then at least praise the one who showed good conduct, such as by saying, 'may Allaah reward you,' because supplication is a means of thankfulness. It is said that whoever's hand is short and cannot recompense should make their tongue long in thankfulness.

A way of thanking people is by not exposing the faults of what was given. Al-Mannaawi, may Allaah have mercy on him, said: "Completeness of thankfulness comprises of hiding the faults of what was given [to you], and not belittling it."[2]

Thankfulness of Allaah the Exalted has been coupled with thankfulness towards people. Abu Hurayrah, may Allaah be pleased with him, said: "Whoever does not thank the people does not thank Allaah."[3] The meaning of the Hadeeth is that Allaah the Exalted does not accept the thankfulness of the slave if they do not thank the people for their good conduct.

---

[1] Reported by Abu Dawood (4813) and Al-Albaani ruled it as being acceptable
[2] Faidh Al-Qadeer (6/22)
[3] Reported by Abu Dawood (4811) and At-Tirmithi (1954) and he said that it is authentic

Either that, or the meaning is that the person whose natural state and custom is to be ungrateful towards people, then their custom will also be to be ungrateful towards the Creator of people.

There are differences between thanking another slave and thanking the Lord. Thanking the Lord consists of submission, humility, and servitude. As for thanking of a slave, then it is to recompense them for their good conduct, and to supplicate for them. It is impermissible to render any submission, humility, or servitude to a slave.

Some of them said: "Thankfulness to He who is above you – meaning Allaah – is by obeying Him, thankfulness towards your peer is through reciprocity, and thankfulness to the one below you is by showing good conduct."[1]

Furthermore, Allaah the Exalted is the One that deserves unconditional and complete thanks. As for thanking a slave, it is a recompense for what good Allaah the Exalted has facilitated through their hand. Therefore, a person should thank their parents for their raising them, their teacher for teaching them, and so forth.[2]

Thanking creation is not an impediment to thanking the Creator, but rather, the problem occurs when people thank the creation and not the Creator, and this is a severe calamity.

---

[1] Rooh Al-Ma`aani (1/258)
[2] Majmoo` Al-Fataawaa (14/339)

Seeking thanks from people:

If a Muslim benefits their brother in a particular manner, it is not befitting to wait for thanks from them, rather, they must wait for the reward and recompense with Allaah. The fact that their brother did not thank them does not mean that their intent was not fulfilled, unless their intent was to acquire the thanks of people, then in that case, they are people of Riyaa' (showing off) and Sum`ah (seeking reputation). We ask Allaah to be saved and upright.

Actually, the scholars have mentioned that if the person who does some sort of good is known to want praise, then it is not befitting for the one who took use of the person's good conduct to praise and thank them, because seeking thanks is injustice, and we have been prohibited from helping in committing injustice.[1]

Ingratitude towards blessings

Kufr (ingratitude) is the opposite of Shukr (thankfulness). Allaah the Exalted has warned us from showing ingratitude towards His Blessings that He has bestowed on us, and the pious predecessors used to be very fearful of being unthankful for blessings.

---

[1] Al-Athkaar by An-Nawawi (pg. 615)

Thankfulness

For example, whenever `Umar ibn `Abdul-`Azeez, may Allaah have mercy upon him, used to look at the blessings that Allaah the Exalted has bestowed on him, he would say: "O Allaah, I seek refuge in You from exchanging Your blessings with ingratitude, denying them after realizing them, or forget them, causing me to not praise You for them."[1]

Some people show ingratitude towards blessings in some situations, and here are some of those situations:

Ingratitude when calamity befalls:

Allaah the Exalted Says (what means): {And if We give man a taste of mercy from Us and then We withdraw it from him, indeed, he is despairing and ungrateful.} [QUR'AAN 11:9] **Ibn Jareer, may Allaah have mercy on him, said: "They are ungrateful towards the One who has bestowed on them, and have little praise for the Lord, who has bestowed on them by what He had given them from His Blessing."[2]**

If the slave knows that every calamity that befalls them is due to their own sins, then they would thank Allaah the Exalted for that, and would blame themselves for their deficiency and negligence. Allaah the Exalted Says (what means): {In order that you not despair over what has eluded you and not exult [in pride] over what He has given you. And Allaah does not like everyone self-deluded and boastful.} [QUR'AAN 57:23]

---

[1] Shu`ab Al-Imaan (4545)
[2] Tafseer At-Tabari (7/9)

Allaah the Exalted has dispraised the person that is ungrateful for their blessings at the time of calamity. When Allaah the Exalted Says (what means): {Indeed mankind, to his Lord, is ungrateful.} [QUR'AAN 100:6] Al-Hasan, may Allaah have mercy on him, explained it, saying: "Meaning, they count their calamities and forget their blessings."[1]

If you look at a businessman today, you find that their income used to be 100,000, but now it is down to 50,000, and if you were to ask them, they would say: 'There are no sales or profits, and we are living in loss!' However, it is obligatory on them to thank Allaah the Exalted in all situations.

This is more frequently seen in women. If you treat a woman well for eternity and for one's whole life, then she sees a shortcoming, she would say: 'I have never seen anything good from you!' This is injustice, and women are most of the inhabitants of Hellfire because they are ungrateful to their husbands. If ungratefulness towards the husband leads to Hellfire, what would be the case of the one who is ungrateful towards the blessings of Allaah?

Patience and thankfulness

Ibn Al-Qayyim, may Allaah have mercy on him, said: "Faith consists of two halves, the first being thankfulness, and the other being patience."[2] The scholars have differences of

---

[1] Tafseer Ibn Katheer (4/700)
[2] Zaad Al-Ma`aad (4/304)

opinion regarding who is better: a poor, patient person, or a rich, thankful person. According to some scholars, thankfulness while being healthy is greater than being patient in wake of trials.

Mutarraf ibn `Abdullaah, may Allaah have mercy on him, said: "To be healthy and thank Allaah the Exalted for my situation is more beloved to me than being tested and remaining patient."[1]

Meaning, if I was given thankfulness in wake of blessings, that is better than being tested and being patient. The Prophet, sallallaahu `alayhi wa sallam, advised that we ask Allaah for forgiveness and wellbeing[2], and did not order us to ask for calamities and patience.

Other scholars said that being patient in the wake of tests and trials is better than being thankful while being safe and healthy. What is apparently correct however, is that both thankfulness and patience are better in their respective situations. So, thankfulness, in respect to the rich person, is better, and patience, in respect to the poor person, is better.

Abu Sahl As-Su`looki, may Allaah be pleased with him, was asked if thankfulness or patience is better, and he replied: "They are equal; thankfulness is necessary during times of ease, and patience is necessary during times of hardship."[3]

---

[1] Musannaf `Abdur-Razzaaq (20468) and Shu`ab Al-Imaan (4435)
[2] Sunan At-Tirmithi (3594) and he ruled it as being acceptable
[3] Ad-Durr Al-Manthoor (1/371)

Thanking for the calamity:

The level that is higher than being patient in wake of calamities is to thank Allaah the Exalted for granting those calamities; calamities are not void of blessings that must be thanked for.
Imaam Al-Haramain Al-Juwaini, may Allaah have mercy on him, said: "Hardships in this life necessitate that the slave thank Allaah for them, because they are actually blessings. The proof is that a slave might be exposed, due to the calamity, to great benefits, abundant reward, and noble matters that make the hardship negligible when compared to them."[1]

Shuraih, may Allaah have mercy on him, said: "A slave has not been afflicted with a calamity except that Allaah blessed them in three ways [in that calamity]: it is not regarding their religion, it is not greater than it was, and that it was inevitably going to happen, and it happened, and is in the past."[2]
If the slave knows this, they would thank Allaah the Exalted that the calamity was not in their religion, was not greater than it was, and should praise and thank Allaah the Exalted that it happened and is in the past.

One of the things that help a person be thankful during times of calamity is to know the good things that result from them, such as rewards that are given to the one who has been afflicted with the calamity.

---

[1] Faidh Al-Qadeer (2/133)
[2] Taareekh Dimashq (23/42)

Thankfulness

> *Al-Ghazaali, may Allaah have mercy on him, said: "Whoever does not believe that the reward of the affliction is greater than the affliction cannot be imagined to be thankful at the time of a calamity."*[1]

Conclusion

Brothers and sisters in Islaam, Allaah the Exalted has bestowed various apparent and hidden blessings and bounties, so, do not associate anything or anyone in worship with Allaah, and direct your thanks and worship to Him alone.

Allaah the Exalted described that those who thank Him from His slaves are few. He the Exalted Says (what means):

- {And few of My servants are grateful.} [QUR'AAN 34:13]
- {And Allaah is full of bounty to the people, but most of the people do not show gratitude.} [QUR'AAN 2:243]

`Umar ibn Al-Khattaab, may Allaah be pleased with him, heard a man saying: "O Allaah, make me from the minority." He said to him: "What is this?" He said: "O commander of the believers, Allaah the Exalted Says (what means): {But none had believed with him, except a few.} [QUR'AAN 11:40] **as well as (what means):** {And few of My servants are grateful.}

---

[1] Ihyaa' `Uloom Ad-Deen (4/131)

Thankfulness

[QUR'AAN 34:13] **as well as (what means):** {Except for those who believe and do righteous deeds - and few are they.} [QUR'AAN 38:24]" `Umar, may Allaah be pleased with him, said: "You have told the truth."[1]

The reason is that Iblees (Satan) has taken it on himself to misguide humanity and prevent them from being thankful. Allaah the Exalted Says informing about him (what means): {Then I will come to them from before them and from behind them and on their right and on their left, and You will not find most of them grateful [to You].} [QUR'AAN 7:17]

Therefore, Iblees knew the importance of the station of thankfulness, and wanted to divert the slaves away from it. Some of them said: "Had Satan known that there was a more virtuous path that leads to Allaah than thankfulness, he would have stood in its path."[2] That is why thankfulness is something hard. Al-Aloosi, may Allaah have mercy on him, said: "It is mentioned that giving Allaah's due of thankfulness is hard, that is why Allaah only praised two of His allies by describing them with thankfulness, and they are Nooh (Noah), may Allaah exalt his mention, and Ibraaheem (Abraham), may Allaah exalt his mention."[3]

Allaah the Exalted Says (what means): {We have certainly created man into hardship.} [QUR'AAN 90:4] **Al-Hasan, may Allaah have mercy on him, said: "They find hardships in**

---

[1] Az-Zuhd by Imaam Ahmad (pg. 114)
[2] Faydh Al-Qadeer (1/526)
[3] Rooh Al-Ma`aani (13/189)

thanking in delightful times, and find hardship in having patience in hard times."[1] Therefore, thankfulness requires struggles and effort.

O Allaah allow us to utter sound speech, to hold fast to Your Book and the Sunnah of Your Prophet, enable us to thank You for what You have bestowed on us, enable us to thank You in a manner that makes You pleased with us, and protect us from the whispers of Iblees (Satan).

Test your understanding

Here are two levels of questions about the topic; there are direct questions, meaning, the first level questions, and questions that need some research and reflection, which are the questions of the second level.

First level questions:

1. What is the difference between praise (Hamd) and thankfulness (Shukr)?
2. There are three meanings for thanks, what are they?
3. What is the rule about talking about the blessings of Allaah the Exalted on you?
4. When it is obligatory to conceal the blessing?
5. There are many evidences that prove that thankfulness is obligatory; mention one piece of evidence for each type of thankfulness.

---

[1] Tafseer Al-Qurtubi (20/56)

6. There are means and ways to achieve thankfulness. What are its most profound ways?
7. Thankfulness is worship, and all worship has fruits. What are the fruits of thankfulness?
8. What is the difference between thanking the Lord and thanking the slave?
9. Who is better: the poor, patient person, or the rich, thankful person?
10. Imaam Ibn Al-Qayyim, may Allaah have mercy on him, spoke about thankfulness and patience in elaboration in one of his books. What is the name of that book?

Second level questions:

1. Ibn Al-Qayyim, may Allaah have mercy on him, said: "Faith consists of two halves, the first being thankfulness, and the other being patience." Explain this statement.
2. During prayer, all three types of thankfulness are exemplified. How could that be the case?
3. Allaah the Exalted Says (what means): {But as for the favor of your Lord, report [it].} [QUR'AAN 93:11]
3. What is meant when Allaah the Exalted Said to inform about the blessings?
4. When does a slave deserve the description that they are thankful for their blessings?
5. Are a slave's thanks for Allaah the Exalted reciprocal?

Thankfulness

6. *"The one who does not thank the people does not thank Allaah."* **Explain this Hadeeth.**
7. **The scholars have mentioned one case wherein it is prohibited to thank people. What is that scenario?**
8. **There are various ways to show ingratitude towards a blessing. What is the greatest of these ways?**
9. *"Shall I not be a slave most thankful."* **What was the incident that caused this Hadeeth?**
10. **Mention two books that talk about thankfulness.**

www.ingramcontent.com/pod-product-compliance
Lightning Source LLC
LaVergne TN
LVHW020442080526
838202LV00055B/5306